For the Children of Derry Church
Past, Present, Future

Unless the Lord builds the house,
those who build it labor in vain.
Psalm 127:1

Copyright © 2024 Derry Church (PCUSA)
Hershey, Pennsylvania
derrypres.org
ISBN: 979-8-35097-203-0
All rights reserved.

Under the Oaks at Derry Church

A Children's Tribute to the 300th Anniversary

Derry Church's 3rd-5th graders (2023-24)
under the direction of
Courtney McKinney-Whitaker and Jill Peckelun

Contributors

Mavis Backenstose
Gavin Cunningham
Kennedy Damron
Vivian DeMartini
Amelia Grudzinski
Harper Grudzinski
Calista June
Riley Knighton
Joanna Kuntch
Brooke Laidler
Emmaline Matthews
Genevieve Minnich
Emi Navarette
Cheyenne Radnor
Carson Santo
Everett Simmons
Ellie Steelman
Lilly Ward
Verity Whitaker

Long Ago

In Irish Gaelic, *doire* (pronounced "deh-ray") means "oak grove."

Long ago in Ireland, people worshiped under oak trees.

In the 1600s, Presbyterians came from Scotland
to the northwestern part of Ireland called Ulster,
where they became known as Ulster Scots.

Many of those Scots Presbyterians
settled in a city called Derry or Londonderry.

Early in the 1700s, many immigrated to North America,
where they became known as the Scots-Irish.

The Session House, Cemetery, and Spring

The earliest members of our church family founded Derry Church
in about 1724 near a spring with a pool of water.
The landscape is important because it gave our church family
what they needed. It's a pretty place. Maybe it felt holy to them.

We wonder how our church family felt
when they came here 300 years ago.
Maybe they felt sad about leaving their homes in Ireland.
Maybe they felt scared to be in a strange new place.

In 1732, they built the Session House.
They used it as a meeting place and a classroom.
Maybe they felt happy to build a community here.

Over time, many of them were buried here.
We like the graveyard because it makes us think of all the people
who had a chance to live on earth and be part of our church family.

Old Derry

During the second half of the 1700s, Derry Church was growing.
In 1769, a new clapboard building went up.
That building served the congregation until 1883.
Today, we call it "Old Derry," but to the people who worshiped there,
it must have been simply Derry Church.

We wonder what it would have been like to worship in that building.
It reminds us of a barn.
Was it cold in the winter?
Did the wind blow through the walls?

After the railroad came in 1858, did the trains shake the building?
Did the people have to wait until the trains passed to hear each other speak, the way we do?

Old Derry Demolished

By the 1870s, Derry Church was going through hard times.
Only a few members remained, and the building was old and unstable.
In 1883, Old Derry was torn down.

We know that the church is the people in it and not the building,
but we still think that must have felt strange and confusing.

Even though the building is gone, parts of Old Derry remain.
The Lord's Table and two chairs in the Chapel came from Old Derry,
and the 1831 pulpit hangs on the wall of the east transept in our Sanctuary.

Each time we take communion, we use the pewter communion set
that the people of Derry Church have used for centuries.
And of course the land remains, with the trees and the birds and the flowers.

It's very special to think that we are still worshiping in the same place
and with some of the same things used by people so many years ago.

The Chapel

In 1883, with only a few members and no building, Derry was in trouble.
Then Derry's friends helped raise over $7,000 for a new stone church.
These friends included the Dauphin County Historical Society
and the Harrisburg Historical Society, who recognized Derry's importance
to the history of the area.

Nearby churches donated money for the stained glass windows,
which honor Derry's pastors from the early years.
On the windows, you can read the names of the churches who helped us.

Because it took a long time to raise the money, building started in 1884,
but the new Memorial Chapel wasn't dedicated until 1887.

The choir and Sunday School met in the west transept
in the Memorial Chapel.
We love to ring the bell in the bell tower!

Faith and Friendship

1917 brought our favorite moment in Derry's history: with profits from
a strawberry festival and bake sales, the Ladies' Guild funded Derry's first indoor toilet!
We are not surprised that the women of the church
were the ones who realized the need for an indoor bathroom.

By 1928, Derry was thinking about renovating the Memorial Chapel.
Only a year later, the Great Depression paused that project.
Again, Derry's friends helped. With loans from the presbytery and the synod,
as well as pledges from members, Derry raised over $25,000. In 1935, the funds were used
for an east transept and four classrooms, plus an assembly room and kitchen in the basement.

That same year, Hershey Chocolate Company founder Milton Hershey gave each church
in the community $20,000 to help out during the Great Depression. Derry used the money
to furnish and equip the new classrooms, renovate the chancel and choir loft,
and add a new pulpit and new carpet. We also got to add a vestibule to the front.
We like to say chocolate saved us!

The story of Derry's Chapel teaches us a lot about faith and friendship,
reminding us that we should accept help when we need it
and help others whenever we can.

The Sanctuary

By 1950, Derry was doing much better.
The Christian Education Building (including Room 6 where we created this book)
was dedicated in 1951. Sunday School was thriving after the
hard years of the Great Depression and World War II. Many of our parents
have told us they came to Derry because it's a good place for children.
Maybe those families felt the same way.

Derry soon outgrew the Chapel. The Sanctuary we worship in today was built in 1965-66.
It looked very different all those years ago. The choir loft was high above the chancel.
All the geometric shapes and the wooden beams
remind us of an optical illusion. It looks very old-fashioned to us,
but we like the way the lights made the dark wood glow.

The Sanctuary Grows

Between 1990 and 1995, the church building got a major makeover.
The Sanctuary got new east and west transepts and a bigger chancel,
so it is now the shape of a cross.
Derry also added a new narthex, lounge, and fellowship hall.

In 2014, Derry added the cross surrounded by a circle of doves. It looks like it's floating
above the Lord's Table. The pulpit and baptismal font were added
in the same year. The design of the metal table legs features Derry's oak leaves
and acorns. We like to look for the birds and squirrels hiding in the branches!

Our Derry Church

When we think of Derry Church, we remember our history.
We remember the people who came here from Ireland,
the people who built Old Derry,
and the people who left us the Chapel and the Sanctuary.
We are thankful for their gift of a beautiful church home.

Derry is a special place where we spend time with our friends and family
and where we make new friends and get to know our church family better.
At Derry, people are kind and welcoming and everyone belongs. We help each other.

As we look toward the future, we hope Derry continues to thrive.
We have learned about Derry's past by creating this book,
and we look forward to helping to build the future of Derry Church.

Our Process

Many people collaborated to produce this book.
The children worked with Jill Peckelun to create the artwork
and with Courtney McKinney-Whitaker to research and compose the text.

We began by reading Bobbie Atkinson's article on the history of Derry Church's buildings
and visiting locations around the church with our sketchpads.
While the children sketched in pencil, Courtney talked to them about their impressions
and interpretations, collecting their language for use in the book. Jill used their sketches
to create composite collages, which the children colored with crayons.
Jill then created new collages from the colored images, while Courtney
composed the text. Children reviewed and revised the drafts.

Pam Whitenack provided ongoing feedback and guidance in our historical understanding
of Derry Church, and Kristy Elliott provided significant classroom support.
Sue George contributed her design skills to put everything together
into the book you're holding now.

Old Derry Church, 1872

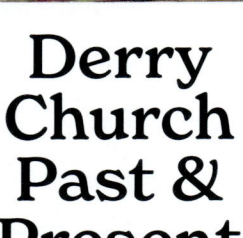

Derry Church Past & Present

Chapel, circa 1890
Built on the site of Old Derry Church

Chapel with Session House in background, 2024

Sanctuary, 1966

Sanctuary interior, 1966

Derry Church, 2024

Draw Your Own Picture of Derry Church